DEAL
with YOUR
SH!T

DEAL

with YOUR

SH!T

---

25 WAYS TO OVERCOME SHAME, HURT, INSECURITIES, AND TRIALS

ERIKA UTLEY, LPC

FOREWORD BY: MILLIE LEE "SINCLAIRE"

Creative Consultant: Mz. Fitch Designs (mzfitchenterprises@gmail.com)
Graphic Designer: IIV Design (www.iivdesign.com)
Editor: Carin Nelson

ISBN: 978-1-982078-38-6

I dedicate this art to all of the people that have experienced emotional turbulence in their lives, in hopes that they will continue to ride the wave.

Peace and Blessings to YOU!

CONTENTS

FOREWORD

Over three decades ago, God sent me a sounding board, someone who would sit for hours, just listening to my crazy problems. Although she was too young to truly comprehend the depth of the issues that plagued me, she listened intently and offered her big sister the best advice she could muster up. She was only around six or seven years old when I found myself sprawled across her therapist couch for the first time. Her juvenile insight became a tool of empowerment for me. I knew that regardless of what ridiculous situation I found myself in, she would always have that same stern answer that caused me to wipe my tears and energized me to go face my problems head on.

As an adult, I have come to realize that I spent many years dumping my trash in my sister's lap. She was my "go-to-gal," my safety net, and the one who sometimes got cut by the broken pieces that life dealt me. How unfair? How selfish? How self-centered? Or was it any of that? It could have been that I did not have the mental, spiritual, nor emotional capacity to deal with the SHIT that had been handed to me, leaving me with only one option at the time, which was to dump it on someone else!!

How many of you are walking around dumping your SHIT on others because you have displaced anger, fear, loneliness, rejection, etc.? That's a real question. Ask yourself, "is that me?" If you answered yes, this book is for you! If you answered no, this book is for you too. This book doesn't discriminate.

Deal with Your SH!T helps you take a deeper dive into the areas of your life that have kept you stagnated, unmotivated, and unfulfilled. It is a practical, easy-read guide that offers over 20 tips for moving

1

beyond your current state to live your optimal life! You will be challenged to flush away toxic people, patterns, and thought processes. You will be pushed to wipe away the pain of your past, the shame of your situations, and the invalid excuses for being mediocre. You will never be the same!

Don't be afraid to get dirty! Don't be too ashamed to get butt naked with your truth! The words penned on the pages within put a bold, in-your-face demand on your life that screams, "Deal with Your SHIT (Shame, Hurt, Insecurities, and Trials)!" No more dragging your garbage around. No more wallowing and, for goodness sakes, no more dumping on others! Let the "Smileologist" — my sister, confidante, and very best friend, Erika Utley, get you right! You deserve it!

-Millie Lee "Sinclaire"

ACKNOWLEDGEMENTS

I have been working on this book in my mind for many years but never quite got it into print version until now. There are many acknowledgments that I could make but that would be another book. So, I will start off with the acknowledgment that has shaped this work of art into what it is. I would like to personally thank my Shame, my Hurt, my Insecurities, and my Trials for making this all possible. Thank you for being there when I didn't even acknowledge your presence. I never knew that it would be you all that would be the foundation of my most sacred work to date. Thank you for making me feel like I wasn't good enough or that I didn't possess the gifts to do this. Without you, I wouldn't be half of the person I am today.

Next, I would like to thank my parents for sacrificing everything for me. Thank you, Mamma and Daddy, for being there with me every step of the way and never giving up on me. I thank you for loving me the best way that you knew how to, even when I was too stubborn to receive it. Thank you for pushing me to be a greater version of myself from the day before. I appreciate you both for seeing the greatness within me and providing opportunities for me to reach my goals. I love you and I thank you for always seeing me beyond my SHIT!

To my siblings, thank you for showing me what to do and in some cases what not to do (lol):

- Rob, I thank you and I love you for always silently cheering for me and always being there to support wherever you could. You have shown me the true definition of what it means to be able to deeply love someone, even if you don't see them every day.

- Pete, thank you for always believing in me and giving me dynamic pointers along the way. You have shown me what a survivor looks like in the face of storms. I thank you for being an example of resiliency in my life. I love you.
- Mildreda, thank you for always pushing me and dropping bright ideas into my spirit. You have been my sister, my mother at times, my best friend, my confidante, and my coach. Thank you for pouring into me even when I didn't want you to. I love you for simply being you.

Thank you to my nephews and niece, Chazz, Josh, Josiah, Mason, and Maya. You guys are truly one of my "whys" - Why I do what I do. You all are one of my greatest inspirations, and I thank you all for that. Keep pressing towards the stars. I love you guys.

I would like to acknowledge my Aunt Carolyn and my cousins, Marlon and Rod. Thank you all for always showing me support and encouraging me along the way. You all have never wavered in your love for me, and for that, I am eternally grateful. I love you all.

I would like to acknowledge my accountability partner, the person who sees me at my best and my worse, and the one who saw this book inside of me before I did. Thank you, Kashia, for pushing me to do and be better. Though at times, I know that my SHIT has been a lot to handle, you have never given up on me. You are my earthly light in my times of darkness. You are a God-sent being, and I am forever grateful to have you in my life. I love you.

Thank you to my bestie, Keira. I want to thank you for always having my back even when the SHIT got tough in my life. Thank you for always stepping in and being who and what I needed you to be at the time. Thank you and I love you for never placing judgment on me but instead loving me through whatever.

Thank you to my furry babies, Prissy and Sweetie, for loving me in a genuine way—Roof-Roof to you guys!

Thank you to every one of my clients that I have serviced over the years, who have taught me humility in knowing that not even a "therapist" is exempt from having issues. I appreciate each and every one of you for unconsciously putting a mirror in my face in an effort for me to pour energy into dealing with my own SHIT.

I would like to thank any person that has ever believed in me. This includes my close friends, my clinical supervisor (Roz), my professors, my colleagues, and the list goes on. Thank you for shining a light on those areas that I didn't even know existed. Those are the same areas that have helped to cultivate this book.

I would also like to give a special thanks to everyone who was a part of actually creating this body of work. I would like to thank my design team for stepping in and bringing my vision to life. I would also like to thank my editor, who agreed to take the job when presented with it at the last minute. Thank you, guys! You all rock!!!

Lastly and most importantly, I thank my Creator. I thank you for giving me life. I thank you for embedding in me secret gifts that I am just now discovering. I thank you for loving me and keeping my mind safe even while dealing with SHIT in my life. I thank you for giving me the creativity to push past all of my pain and share the good news of healing with others. I simply thank you for allowing me the freedom to be ALL that you created me to be.

Erika Utley, LPC

INTRODUCTION

Disclaimer: If you came here expecting to indulge in a body of work that will challenge your intellect and have you running to your dictionary or encyclopedia to gain answers, this is not the book for you. Or, if you picked this book up looking for the error-free work of an English professor, you probably need to exit immediately. Or, if you came here to find political correctness, run now! But if you came here in hopes to begin to put the basic pieces of your emotions back together in a rather simplistic manner, then great. Or, if you came here to finally look in the mirror and address that little girl or little boy in you that has not yet healed, then, CONGRATULATIONS — you are in the right place! In this book, if applied genuinely, you will learn to finally DEAL with your SHIT! Some may ask, "What is SHIT and how do I know if I have SHIT to deal with?" Well, for those of you that asked, I'm glad you did. For the purposes of this book, we will dissect the word SHIT in acronym style to help you determine if you possess SHIT in your life:

The "S" in SHIT represents our SHAME. The most basic definition of shame is an internal feeling of being inadequate somewhere deep down in the core of our being. It is the shame within us that ignites embarrassment or guilt. It is also shame that turns up the volume on the little voice inside of us that tells us that we must always strive for perfection. Shame is a feeling that will cause us to not flow freely into who we truly are or aspire to become. With shame comes hiding and with hiding comes a never-ending life of secrecy. But what if I told you that shame is a choice? For most of us, while we learned shame from negative messages that we received in childhood, it is, in fact, a choice to live with it. We have the choice to continue to validate those early messages daily or begin to create our own messages to live by. What if I also told you that the very people that you hide from deal or have dealt with shame on some level as well? I may be making a far jump here, but it is my belief that no one is exempt from feeling shame at some point in their life. Whether we felt shame because we ran for class president in 5th grade and we didn't make the cut or if we simply slipped and fell in a crowd of people on a rainy day, shame has peeked out its ugly little head at some time or another in all our lives. We have all fallen short before, and none of us are dripping with perfection. With that being said, it brings me to the conclusion that we don't have to feel shame. We can choose to see our experiences that usually evoke the feeling of shame as a) an opportunity to become closer to our true selves and continue evolving or b) an opportunity to run from our self and others, stunting personal growth. The choice is ours!

The "H" in SHIT represents our HURT. When we think of hurt, we typically think of two different manifestations of it - Physical or Emotional Hurt. What we are dealing with here is the emotional hurt in our lives. I have, and most of you have probably said, the following words, "My feelings are hurt." But what exactly does that mean when we say that? I think the most appropriate way to explain those words is by saying that one feels an emotional rupture and perceives it as being inflicted on them by another person/situation. Our feelings of emotional hurt can date back to early events in our lives and if left unresolved, we will surely continue to witness the same hurts in another form as adults. Dealing with hurt is not always the easiest. It means we sometimes have to dig back up what we think is dead, but in all actuality is very much so still living in us. Hurt feelings have historically been the force of why people may make certain choices in their lives. For instance, if I got my feelings hurt after being rejected for a particular job, I would either run far away from applying for the same kind of job again to escape the possible hurt or I may continue to apply for the same job because my ego won't let me have it any other way. Whatever the choice is, we will more times than none find hurt feelings at the core of many decisions that we make, whether good or bad. Because hurt will show up at some point (even for those who have their egos all the way in check), we have to determine what we will do with the hurt. Will we let it fester into hatred and negativity or will we allow it to fuel the greatness that is within all of us?

The "I" in SHIT represents our INSECURITIES. Having insecurities mean having uncertainties and doubts about oneself. In our new day of social media guiding the majority of our leisure time, being secure is somewhat of a foreign concept. We are told by social media WHO to be. Through our daily clicking and downloading in the social media world, we are told what is beautiful and what is handsome. We are also schooled on what it means to be successful and what it takes to get there. We are told that we are "not awesome" if we don't possess certain qualities, enter into specific types of relationships, and achieve outlined milestones by a particular age. Basically, we allow ourselves to be placed in a box, and if we can't have the life that social media suggests, then our box is sealed up and shipped away to "insecurity land." Just imagine if that same person who looks on social media and finds out that he or she is not that awesome, is the same person that lived in an insecurity-breeding home as a child. This person was told by his or her parents then that they were less than worthy and now they are being fed the same message by society. This is how insecurity continues to manifest in our lives. If we never address the messages that we received as a child, we will carry those same messages into our adult lives. Those same insecurities are the building blocks of low self-esteem, failed relationships, and not living purposefully on purpose.

The "T" in SHIT represents our TRIALS. Have you ever been at a place in life where everywhere you turn there is a mountain to climb? You get to one mountain and conquer it, only to find that there's another mountain right behind it. These mountains are better known as our trials. There are only two things one can do when faced with these mountains. One can say "forget this mountain stuff, I'm just going to stay right here and whatever happens, happens." Or one can take some time to re-group, apply all that was learned from climbing the last mountain, and keeping moving. I would hope that we would all be the latter mountain climber described though. There was no memo or public service announcement sent out at the time of our births that said, "Attention, there will be no trials in your life." With that, we all have trials that we will experience. The focus is not on the actual trial though. The focus is on how we respond to it. Will we keep climbing the mountains or will we just become one with the mountain? It would be unreal to say that we should be happy and excited when we have to deal with trials in our lives. But I will say that there should be peace in knowing that we have conquered the mountain before, which provides a reference point that it can be done again and again. It's all about perspective. What type of mountain climber will you be?

So now that you have an understanding of what SHIT really means, do you have any SHIT to DEAL with? If so, I invite you on this journey with me through the next pages in this book. A few things you will need for this journey are:

1.   Alone time - This will not work if you are in the direct presence of different energies. We only need your energy during this time so that the focus can be inward and not outward. Silence all phones, TVs,

spouses, babies, etc. (you may even want to wait until everyone is asleep).

2.   Pen - There will be writing associated with the experience. Don't be afraid to journal the journey. There will be space provided for you to write in the book, but you may decide to use additional paper just in case you want to get rid of the writings afterward (for God's sake, don't throw away the book though).

3.   No Tissues - Do NOT, I repeat, Do NOT reach for tissues if emotions seem to overtake you during this process. The tissues will help you to wipe away the tears, but they will psychologically signal to your brain to stop feeling whatever is causing the pain. However, your healing is in those tears. Let the tears fall where they may.

4.   An Open Mind - Don't be afraid to be vulnerable with yourself during this experience. Be open to yourself and the possibilities. Trust yourself and trust your feelings. You are safe with you!

5.   A Mirror - During the course of this journey, you need to be able to look into your own self for answers. You need this mirror to reflect the true you. This mirror will help you to finally address your inner child that you have been desperately running from and gain victory over your past. This mirror will also allow you to see the beauty in who you truly are today.

Now that we've gotten the housekeeping rules out of the way (and hopefully understood), I am excited to present to you 25 ways to overcome your Shame, Hurt, Insecurities, and Trials! Proceed WITHOUT caution!

Erika Utley, LPC

1. BE HONEST WITH YOURSELF

Can you imagine showing up in a public place completely naked? Can you imagine all of the foul comments and disgraced looks you would receive because you are behaving out of the "norm?" Can you imagine being arrested and taken to jail by legal authorities because you decided not to wear clothes that day? Being naked physically in public places or even at home (except for in the shower), is thought of to be a "no-no." This same notion applies to being naked emotionally. Due to our SHIT, most of us are not naked emotionally. We go to great lengths to stay clothed and not be honest with others and especially ourselves - we tend to dress up our SHIT! We know how to put on the right color, with the perfect design, tailored to camouflage our SHIT. When does this get old to us though? When will we begin to realize that faking our truths only get us so far? We will never get to true purpose, if we are being a "phony" and especially when we are being phony to ourselves.

It is imperative to know that honesty is the cornerstone of healing. If we choose to continue to play "dress up" with our true emotions, healing never takes place. In order to heal, we must travel to those places within us that we have "skillfully" escaped from. Honesty with oneself involves looking in the mirror and being okay with who you see outwardly and inwardly. It also involves evaluating yourself and determining your good, bad, ugly, and indifferent and once again being okay with you. Let's not confuse being okay with you as being stagnant and not putting in work for growth. Saying that you are okay with you is saying, "I understand where I am, I accept where I am, and

13

I am willing to do my work to move to the next level." It is not saying, "I accept myself and I cannot change myself."

By being honest with ourselves, we begin to embark on emotional maturity. Being dishonest with ourselves causes us to sustain an elementary level of emotional maturity. This lack of maturity manifests itself in being in relationships that we don't even want to be in, working jobs that we absolutely despise, and just simply enmeshing ourselves into things that are the furthest from the representation of our truth. We have to be honest with ourselves and put away these masks that have crippled us for so many years. We have to understand that OUR truth will set us free within!

DEAL WITH YOUR SH!T

Use the spaces below to write your TRUTH - be honest - and keep in mind, that only you know your truth, so don't try to do anyone any favors by formulating something other than the truth...

_____

_____

_____

_____

_____

_____

_____

_____

_____

_____

_____

_____

_____

_____

_____

_____

_____

Erika Utley, LPC

2. ACCEPT YOUR TRUTH

Once we know our truth, the work then is accepting our truth. We have to learn that our truth is who we are. If we don't accept our truth, we are not accepting of ourselves. The sad reality is that many of us don't want to accept our truth. We would rather know the truth but continue to run from it not realizing that it will only keep running behind us.

Our truth is a powerful force and will show up even when you think that you have done a tremendous job at keeping it tucked away. When I was growing up, one of the famous lines in my household was, "whatever you do in the dark, will always come to light." And as aggravating as that line was as a child, I found it to be nothing less than accurate since I have lived life a little. But I want to take it a step further here and say, "whatever you don't accept as your dark, will always come and dim your light." This basically means that when we go through hoops to tuck away and not accept our truth, it will always show up even in those times where life seems to be going just the way we desire. For example, imagine you married a person and they literally made all of your dreams come true. They possessed every quality that you ever wrote down in your journal as a "must have" for your future spouse. Everything is great until one day, you realize that you are not able to be physically intimate with your partner. Every instance of intimacy makes you sick to your stomach, but you force yourself to be in the act and attempt to enjoy it. Your truth is that you were sexually molested as a child, and the mere act of being vulnerable intimately brings about discomfort and uncertainty. You know why you are unable to be intimate with your dream-come-true spouse, but you have not ACCEPTED your truth.

If you do not accept your truth, the dark parts of you will begin to overshadow the light within you. The goal is to accept your truth and know that acceptance allows the journey of healing to begin. It allows you to face your truth and, as stated previously, be okay with it. When it comes to acceptance, you must determine what that looks like for you personally. For some, it could mean forgiving another person, for another, it could mean no longer living in regret, and for someone else, it could simply mean living life with no expectations. It is up to you to define and live out what acceptance of your truth is.

DEAL WITH YOUR SH!T

Below, write about the truths that you have not accepted up to this point in life:

_____

_____

_____

_____

_____

_____

_____

_____

_____

_____

_____

_____

_____

_____

_____

_____

_____

_____

Erika Utley, LPC

3. LET THE DUST SETTLE

After you become aware and accepting of your SHIT, the next tip is to simply "let the dust settle." In a world where we are not actually taught to deal with our emotions, we usually find ourselves attempting to escape from them. Society has created so many outlets and products to help us numb our SHIT that most times, that is exactly what we do when we should be dealing with our feelings instead.

It is okay to have a moment with yourself. It is also okay to deal with the feelings associated with your shame, hurt, insecurities, and trials without trying to alleviate the pain. Welcome the feelings into your world. Do not abandon them. Do not tell them, "Hey I will deal with you at some other point." If the feelings come knocking at your door, invite them in. Offer them a seat on your couch and tell them that you are glad that they stopped by. Talk with your feelings. Tell them how they help you to remember that you are, in fact, human. Don't be afraid to also tell your feelings why you have run from them for so long. Be okay with letting them know that you were once afraid of them, but that is no longer true. And lastly, tell them that they are welcomed anytime. This is how you let the dust settle after owning and accepting your truth!

Be okay with feeling because, in order to heal, we must FEEL. Am I suggesting that you allow your feelings to be a roommate instead of an overnight guest in your emotional home? No, not at all... What I am saying is to welcome your feelings when they arise. Don't shut them out because — just like the annoying salesman that knocks on your door consistently no matter how much you tell them "no thank you" — your feelings will do the same. Have your moment and let the dust settle...

DEAL WITH YOUR SH!T

Write about those feelings that you have tried to escape, then afterwards, sit with them...

_____

_____

_____

_____

_____

_____

_____

_____

_____

_____

_____

_____

_____

_____

_____

_____

Erika Utley, LPC

4. MAKE PEACE WITH YOUR PAST

Peace is essentially a gift that we all have been afforded to have within us. It is the load of our SHIT that causes us to forget that inner peace. Our inner peace is covered with the tons and tons of shame, hurt, insecurities, and trials that we carry within us day after day after day. We forget that we have the power to simply LET IT GO.

We allow faulty thinking to cause us to feel that the past is the most important part of us and there is no way to move forward without carrying it with us. This thinking is absurd! The day you choose to look your past square in the eyes and say, "Enough of you, I accept you, and I am at peace with you," is the day that the walls of your mental bondage will come tumbling down. Make peace with the past, knowing that every experience was put in place to teach you more about the greatness that will soon erupt from you.

Yes, that person hurt you! And yes, you were only an innocent child! Yes, you were abandoned and left all alone. And yes, they teased you for simply being you! But here's the part to run and do a cartwheel about... No, you weren't defeated even though they hurt you. And no, you didn't give up on life even though you were only a child! No, you didn't stop fighting for your life even though you were abandoned and left all alone! And no, you never stopped loving yourself even though they teased you.

Making peace with your past is about reframing your thoughts about it. It's about looking at the facts of what occurred but also rejoicing in the fact that you still have the opportunity to find the lesson attached to each experience. The lessons learned will move you closer to your destined purpose. Our feelings associated with our past should not be discredited, but they should instead be evaluated. We need to understand why we feel they way we do about our past and determine if we are open to letting the feelings go. Some of us are not open to letting go because the pain of the past is familiar and it brings comfort. But sometimes we must determine if being comfortable is more important than truly living on purpose, even if it is uncomfortable for a while.

Growth doesn't take place in an environment of comfort. We have the choice to make peace with our past and, as always, we must determine what doing that looks like for us. Does it mean writing a letter to someone forgiving them or does it mean looking in the mirror and forgiving oneself?

DEAL WITH YOUR SH!T

Making peace with the past looks different for different people. What does it truly look like for you?

_____

_____

_____

_____

_____

_____

_____

_____

_____

_____

_____

_____

_____

_____

_____

_____

_____

_____

_____

_____

Erika Utley, LPC

5. FIGURE OUT YOUR OWN PERSONAL AGREEMENTS

From the time we are born and probably up until this very moment, we may find ourselves living by agreements that we did not particularly decide to enter into. When we are younger, we are born into families where the standards and practices have already been put into place. Our parents or caretakers are the first people to strip our mental freedom from us. They determine the name that we will be called for the rest of our lives, they control the foods we consume, they dictate where we will live, and overall, they enforce what it is that we are to believe in. Now, before we go any further, please note that these are just examples — I'm not telling you to run down to your state government office and do a name change tomorrow (unless you absolutely don't agree with your name). This is more so for you to begin to create your own agreements, separate from the ones that were given to you up until this point.

If you grew up in a Catholic home and now you feel like you are connected to the Buddhist faith, then it is encouraged that you begin to explore your own agreements. If you grew up in a home where being attracted to the same sex was forbidden but you know your truth is that you are in fact attracted to another man or women, it is encouraged that you begin to formulate your own agreements. If you grew up in a home where consuming alcohol or drugs was the daily routine and you find that not to be a true representation of who you are, it may be time to create your own agreements. All too often, we are living with the agreements that others have made for us. This causes us to deny ourselves, as adults, to truly make our own choices. We find it hard to detach from what "was" and attach to what truly "is."

Will some people not agree with the agreements you put in place for yourself? Abso-freakin-lutely, but that's not your issue - that's their issue. In order to live your most authentic life, evaluate your current agreements, throw out the ones you don't genuinely agree with, and begin to insert new personal agreements as needed.

DEAL WITH YOUR SH!T

What are agreements that you have in your life that you don't necessarily agree with? Where did the agreements originate from? What are some of your new agreements that you have created?

Erika Utley, LPC

6. TEND TO YOUR GARDEN

Our lives are similar to gardens—different seeds are planted and these seeds will either grow if tended to properly or they will die with lack of proper care. Sometimes seeds are planted that may not be the best fit for our garden, and sometimes seeds are planted that will cause our garden to grow in an abundance of greatness. So let's go back to the beginning of how our gardens began. While we were in the womb, seeds were being planted within us. Whether our parents were joyful and loving towards us, or if they were resentful the entire time of us forming, seeds were being planted.

Let's use two different scenarios here. We have the mother and father who became pregnant with who we will call "Child A." When Child A's parents found out that there was a baby on the way, they were filled with so much joy and happiness. They immediately began to tell family members and friends about their new bundle of joy on the way. Every night before the parents would go to sleep, they would talk to the unborn child and tell it how much they loved it over and over again. Now back to the garden - the parents' confession of love to their unborn child planted the first seed in Child A's life. This seed is called LOVE. Now let's discuss the second scenario with who we will call "Child B." Child B was born to parents that conceived it after having a one-night stand with one another. When the mother found out that she was expecting a child, she immediately became angry and told the doctor that she didn't want a baby. The mother of Child B attempted to reach out to the father, but he shared that he was married and was not about to let a random baby mess up his happy home. Now back to the garden—the parents' bitterness and resentment toward the unborn child planted the first seed in Child B's life. This seed is called REJECTION.

So as we can see, our gardens are created even before we take our first breath outside of the womb. We come here with no idea of the seeds that will be planted in our lives; however, once we begin to face our truth, we can begin to sort out the seeds in our gardens. We can determine what to pull up and what to keep. Let it also be known that if you do not tend to your own garden, you will possibly chance planting the same seeds that caused some of your SHIT into the gardens of your own children. For instance, if you never deal with your insecurities, you will possibly plant those same insecurities into your offspring. I wouldn't be surprised if you share some of the same insecurities that your mother or father have or had. It's time to clean up the garden in order to grow abundantly in your life.

What seeds were planted in your life as a child? Are you still watering those same seeds?

_____

_____

_____

_____

_____

_____

_____

_____

_____

_____

_____

_____

_____

_____

_____

_____

_____

_____

_____

Erika Utley, LPC

7. IDENTIFY YOUR CRUTCHES

I will never forget when I was a kid and I had a family member who had recently been in an accident. I remember we had walking aids (walkers, crutches, etc.) in the basement of our home. When I knew that everyone was busy doing something else, I would go down there and go straight to the crutches and begin to play with them. I was amazed at how I could hold one of my legs up and still walk while the crutches held me up. I just couldn't believe that they made walking that easy and that I didn't have to put all the pressure on my own legs to get around. I was in love with those crutches, as strange as that may sound. When I think of those crutches in my childhood basement, I begin to think about the crutches we use, to help us not deal with our SHIT. I think about how having crutches makes it easier, and we don't have to really put in work.

One of the main crutches that we lean on in life is relationships. We get into relationships with the hope that they can either fill the void from our SHIT or we hope that the relationship itself will carry us through life, which means never having to face our SHIT. Either way, relationships are usually the crutch that most of us can relate to. We think that other people can fix things for us and that is the furthest from the truth. We have to do our own work, and the relationships should only be an added bonus to our lives. So, if you are in a relationship and you are using someone to fill a void or using them to avoid your SHIT altogether, good luck to you. It's human nature to desire companionship, but it is not human nature to use relationships to avoid your SHIT.

Other crutches that we tend to use to not deal with our SHIT are substances, such as drugs and alcohol. You would be amazed (or maybe not) at the percentage of people that use these substances daily to attempt to cope with their shame, hurt, insecurities, and trials. Being that I have tried both, I can tell you that they don't do an absolute thing in the long run for your emotional freedom. What they will do, though, is prolong your healing process. Drugs and alcohol are crutches that, if you are not careful, can appear to be the best friend you never had. I say this because these substances don't talk back, they listen, and they never tell you NO. If you are truly ready to walk on your own again, drop the crutches to the side and move forward!

DEAL WITH YOUR SH!T

What are some of the crutches that you use in your life?

_____

_____

_____

_____

_____

_____

_____

_____

_____

_____

_____

_____

_____

_____

_____

_____

_____

_____

Erika Utley, LPC

8. LEARN TO SAY NO

Sometimes it is so difficult for us to tell someone NO. We find it hard to potentially be a disappointment to someone. Therefore, we agree to something that we know deep-down inside we do NOT want to even be a part of. Have you ever attended an event and knew that you would have been happier snuggled up under your blanket, binge-watching your favorite Netflix series? Well, if you haven't, I definitely have, and I must admit that those times have been some of the most dreadful times of my life. When I look back, I could have just said, "NO, I think I am going to stay in tonight but happy birthday anyway," or "NO, I won't be able to attend but congrats on your graduation." But because of my need to please, I agreed to do something that my entire being didn't truly want to do.

I attribute my not saying NO due to me not having dealt with my own SHIT at that time. If my insecurity of not being good enough had not kicked in, I would have gladly said NO and would not have thought twice about someone actually thinking that I was a lesser person if I didn't attend their shindig. It would have been water under the bridge, and I would have been able to kick back and do what I wanted to do, which essentially was nothing. But it would have been my prerogative to do that.

Learn to say NO, especially when your heart and spirit say "no." The people you say NO to will be okay, and if they aren't and they want to throw you out of their life, then that's their business. Be sure enough in knowing that you have every right to say NO.

DEAL WITH YOUR SH!T

When have you been unable to say NO? How did you feel about it?

_____

_____

_____

_____

_____

_____

_____

_____

_____

_____

_____

_____

_____

_____

_____

_____

_____

_____

_____

Erika Utley, LPC

9. LEARN TO SAY YES

The opposite of learning to say no is learning to say YES! Sometimes, fear will creep in and soon to follow is insecurity that will tell us, "You can't do that," or "You know you need to stay in your lane, that is not for you." Well, if you listen to those insecurities, you will always find yourself saying no to opportunities and more importantly, possibilities.

When in search of our true selves, we must go through trial and error. We must learn what makes us tick, we must learn what is not necessarily a gift that we possess, and we must learn to not back down from opportunities. But we will never learn these things if we never say YES. I remember some time ago being asked to come in for a job interview for a position that I insecurely felt unqualified for. I remember going back and forth in my mind asking myself, should I even go to the interview—given that my resume was not at all what the employer asked for as far as experience and skills. I finally decided to attend the interview and, to my surprise, I was offered the job. After the offer was placed on the table, my insecurities kicked in again and had me questioning whether or not I should even accept the offer. I eventually made up my mind and decided to say, "YES!" That was the YES that cultivated my ability to say yes even today.

Within the first three months of being on that job, my choice to say YES led me to receive a very nice increase in my pay, due to my outstanding performance. Now, remember, this was the job I questioned whether or not I was qualified to do—this should show you that saying YES is, more often than not, a sure way to receive growth in one way or another. Kick your SHIT aside and learn to say YES! You never will know what is on the other side of YES if you are too afraid to say it.

When have you said YES, and what was the outcome?

_____

_____

_____

_____

_____

_____

_____

_____

_____

_____

_____

_____

_____

_____

_____

_____

_____

_____

_____

_____

Erika Utley, LPC

10. CONNECT TO YOUR CREATOR

Great debaters have often discussed where we came from and how it all began. Some people believe that we were created from dust and formed in the image of our Creator, and some may believe that we were created and genetically engineered by an alien. Whatever our belief may be as it relates to creation, we should have a connection to that belief.

If we don't have a connection to our Creator, how do we begin to ask all the questions that we need to ask about our existence? You, as the creation, wouldn't know why you were created. All you would know is that you are here and that some force created you. So how do we move in the direction we should, if we do not have true connection and communication with our Creator? The answer is clear, we don't move in the direction that we should, because we are depending solely on ourselves for all the answers.

Newsflash... if you had all of the answers, you wouldn't be reading this book. So there you have it, connect to your Creator. Not only can you ask the "whys" but you can also begin to put a little bug in the ear of your Creator, asking for your "wants." Once you do that, STAND IN EXPECTANCY. If you were created, know that you were created with purpose. It is on us to clear out our SHIT so that we can get back in tune with our CREATOR in the purest style.

What are your thoughts on how you were created? What are the questions that you have for your Creator? What are the things that you plan to stand in expectancy for?

_____

_____

_____

_____

_____

_____

_____

_____

_____

_____

_____

_____

_____

_____

_____

_____

_____

_____

11. BE YOUR OWN BEST FRIEND

Spending time alone is one of the most therapeutic experiences ever known to the "conscious" man. Being by yourself allows for you to hear only your thoughts without the interference of another person's thoughts. In spending time with oneself, we learn to discover our true selves without the noise of the outside world.

For some of us though, being alone presents much anxiety. We make it our business to fill our schedules up with activities that will include the energies of others. Why is this so? Well, the answer is simple, we know that if we are alone, we are forced to deal with our SHIT and we don't always want to do that. We look to others to provide distractions and never even fully get to know who we are. We intertwine ourselves into the being of someone else because it seems to be easier. Well, what happens when that person is no longer available? Or if that cooking class that you faithfully attend every Monday and Wednesday discontinues the program? You would be left to deal on your own.

I can't tell you how many times I was in a relationship and the other party decided to leave. I mean, my world was turned upside down because I didn't know how to be in my own company. I was so comfortable with depending on the essence of another person to validate my being, and this was a recipe for disaster. Once I learned this concept (after many failed relationships), it clicked that I have to be my own best friend. I learned that I have to enjoy me. It became evident to me that I was living a life of co-dependency, and it was because I did not want to deal with my SHIT.

With that being said, don't wait until later to begin to love on your own damn self. Begin today! Don't wait for the presence of another being to validate who you are because you will be waiting forever. I encourage you to be your own best friend. Take yourself out on dates. Tap into new hobbies. Learn to meditate on your own thoughts. Find the beauty within you and allow it to exude from the inside out. You can only do these things if you decide to silence the outer chatter and go within for all of your answers. This, my friend, will lead you down the path of SELF AWARENESS, which promotes healing.

What are some qualities that you like about yourself? What are some things that you could improve about yourself? How will you become your own BFF?

_____

_____

_____

_____

_____

_____

_____

_____

_____

_____

_____

_____

_____

_____

_____

_____

_____

_____

Erika Utley, LPC

12. GIVE ONLY FROM YOUR OVERFLOW

Are you guilty of trying to do something for someone else that you haven't even done for yourself? Do you find yourself trying to give something to someone you love when you don't really even have anything to give? Well, if you answered "yes" to one or both of those questions, listen up. Give only from your OVERFLOW. It is downright insane to try to feed your neighbor when you haven't had a morsel of food in days. To some, this would be called an act of selflessness, but to me, this is an act of selfishness.

How do you try and breathe for someone else when you are running out of oxygen yourself? This is selfish to your own self. The goal is to take care of oneself first, in an effort to be able to care for someone else later (if you have the means to do so). I absolutely love traveling, but the plane rides always bring a bit of anxiety into my inner spirit, which is probably the same for many people. We get on this plane and before we take off, the flight attendants give us a long list of rules "just in case" there's a life-threatening emergency. If that doesn't cause anxiety, I don't know what does... but let me get back on track. One of the main rules that the announcer tells all passengers is, "In case of a sudden drop in cabin pressure, an oxygen mask will automatically appear in front of you. To start the flow of oxygen, pull masks toward you and place it over your nose and mouth. If you are traveling with someone else, please be sure to secure your mask first, then assist the other person." Wow - aha moment! That means, save yourself first, and then work to possibly save someone else. If you attempt to do the reverse and try to help get the oxygen mask on your neighbor first, you will be staring death in the face while you're losing your own oxygen. This is backwards on so many levels.

Doesn't it make so much more sense to take care of yourself first, so that you will have the energy to assist someone else? Easy concept, but truly challenging for those of us that have not learned to value oneself... I would be willing to bet my life that this "selfless" person hasn't dealt with their SHIT yet...

DEAL WITH YOUR SH!T

Are you okay with saving yourself first? If not, why? What do you have stored up in your overflow to give to others?

_____

_____

_____

_____

_____

_____

_____

_____

_____

_____

_____

_____

_____

_____

_____

_____

_____

Erika Utley, LPC

13. KNOW THAT PEOPLE CAN ONLY GIVE WHAT THEY HAVE

You wake up and realize that you are in the back of an ambulance, laid out on a stretcher. You have absolutely no movement of your neck, due to having a terribly uncomfortable brace on. You look down at your chest and you see that you are bleeding profusely and can only speculate that you may have been shot. When you finally look in front of you to see who you are under the care of, to your surprise, you see a person in a dirty jumpsuit, filled with car grease and other unimaginable substances, standing in front of you with a wrench in one hand and pliers in the other. You realize in that moment that this person is a mechanic and not medical personnel. This person is only equipped to fix cars and surely cannot help you in this time of need. What do you do?

Well, I guess this situation is a little more extreme than where I am going with it, but I needed you to get a visual of a person only being able to give you what he or she is equipped with. The only thing you can do is accept the equipment that the person comes with. Many times, we find ourselves having expectations for other people. We want them to love us a certain kind of way. We want them to protect us in times of distress. We may even want them to deal with our SHIT for us. However, if the person is not equipped with those qualities, then we must accept it.

Growing up, I desired being told how beautiful, smart, and talented that I was. I wanted to accomplish something and feel the joy of knowing that I made someone proud. But guess what, that didn't happen. It wasn't until I got older that I understood that I could only receive from people the things that they were equipped with. It became crystal clear that the things that I needed emotionally were not intentionally left unnoticed, but instead, the people I needed them from could not give them to me. Why? Because they weren't equipped with showing love and support in the way that I needed it.

In the above scenario with the mechanic in the back of the ambulance, you couldn't have an expectation for him to save your life. The mechanic can ONLY bring to the table what he is equipped with - no more, no less. So, in dealing with your SHIT, it may be time to look at those people you resent for not being there the way you needed them to. They may have just been a mechanic in a medical worker's world.

DEAL WITH YOUR SH!T

Do you hold resentment towards someone for not being there the way you needed them to be? Was this person truly equipped to handle and deliver your need?

_____

_____

_____

_____

_____

_____

_____

_____

_____

_____

_____

_____

_____

_____

_____

Erika Utley, LPC

14. STOP PLAYING THE BLAME GAME

It is human nature of our egos to not want to be wrong. As a result, we can find ourselves playing the blame game. We point the finger at "him," "her," and "it," and never take accountability for the part we play in our SHIT. If you have been hurt by others, I truly do hope that you will learn forgiveness and apply the steps that you are learning in this book to move forward.

However, if you choose to continue to live in hurt, that is truly your fault. You will no longer be able to blame other people for your SHIT. You have gotten away with it thus far, but today, we take the training wheels off. We begin to see life for what it truly is. We will work on making peace with the past and begin to place our focus on the here and now. NO ONE, and I repeat, NO ONE is responsible for your SHIT but you.

It is so much easier to shift the blame onto others and become detached from our issues without ever dealing with them. This concept can be confusing slightly because people in our lives have had a helping hand in causing our shame, hurt, insecurities, and trials. However, it is not their fault if you choose to continue to allow your SHIT to stay alive. We can only put the flame out when we chose to face our own selves. Blaming will never help us deal. Blame will only serve as a bandage and will cause us to never fully heal. Take that bandage off and DEAL with your SHIT!

Do you find yourself blaming others for the mental state that you are in? Name some of those situations.

_____

_____

_____

_____

_____

_____

_____

_____

_____

_____

_____

_____

_____

_____

_____

_____

15. LIVE IN THE PRESENT MOMENT

When I get in my car to drive, one of the first things that I do is adjust my rearview mirror. I do this so that I can look back (if needed) to avoid any potential danger. What would my drive be like if I looked in my rearview mirror the entire time that I was driving? Yes, you are correct, I would probably crash.

This same situation is important to apply in our emotional lives. If we continue to look back at our past, we will miss the importance of everything that is right in our present view. If we are so stuck on the things behind us, we may risk missing out on that possibility of a lifetime. The only thing that we should do with our past is look back just for quick reference points. We are not to stay there. If there was a situation from your past that you have overcome, you may need a little reminder that you are a conqueror and looking back to provide this reminder is quite all right. Just like in the car, we can look in the rearview mirror just to avoid any potential danger.

The other part to living in the present moment is to not focus so much on the future either. What if the future never comes and you have wasted all of your precious time missing out on your present? For those of us that take road trips, we know that there are two different types of road trippers. There are the road trippers that keep their focus straight ahead, never looking off to the side of them to maybe see beautiful flowers, or a breathtaking body of water, or hell, even witnessing a cow giving birth. Their focus is on the destination and not the journey of getting there. Then you have road trippers that look at everything around them while traveling. They even notice that in 2.5 miles, there will be a sale on fresh fruit and veggies. These type of road trippers focus on the present moment, and when they get to their destination, they get to their destination— there's no rush. You must determine which road tripper you will be.

Are you focused on the past or the future and not basking in the present beauties of life? Or are you soaking up every moment and relinquishing control of your future? Explain...

_____

_____

_____

_____

_____

_____

_____

_____

_____

_____

_____

_____

_____

_____

_____

_____

Erika Utley, LPC

16. KNOW YOUR OWN WORTH

Knowing your own worth is understanding your own greatness even in the absence of the validation from others. We must learn to become so in tune with ourselves that we begin to embrace the fact that we are not like any other creature out there. We were created with purpose that only we—not anyone else—can manifest. That in itself should be a constant reminder of the great levels of worth that we individually have.

Unfortunately, when we allow our SHIT to cloud our thinking, we begin to see ourselves as less than who we were created to be. We begin to search for our greatness in the hearts of others, and this will never truly work. It is not another person's duty to define what your worth is— it is solely up to you. The other person is unable to show you your worth, as they should be busy defining their own sense of self-worth. You are responsible for valuing and loving yourself. Yes, it is a plus if someone would like to come along and add even more love and value to our lives, but just in case they don't, you will be prepared to do it all on your own. That way, no one can ever subtract from your value if they wake up one morning and decide to leave, never to return. If you are the author and finisher of your own worth, then it is a permanent value and cannot ever be altered by others. It is important that we begin to see ourselves as a unique being and focus on the way in which we will move and operate in that uniqueness. That same uniqueness will help you to embrace the SHIT you've been through and eventually lead you to a lifetime of limitless self-acceptance and self-love.

69

What makes you worthy? What makes you a valuable, unique individual?

_____

_____

_____

_____

_____

_____

_____

_____

_____

_____

_____

_____

_____

_____

_____

_____

_____

17. EVALUATE YOURSELF DAILY

One way to determine if you are really starting to deal with your SHIT is by evaluating yourself daily. Make it a practice at the end of your day, probably right before bed, to evaluate the day and your involvement in it. Based upon your personal agreements, determine everything you did right during the day, determine everything you did wrong during the day, and determine ways to become more of who you are the next day. This evaluation of yourself will also help you to determine your motives for why you did what you did in a given day.

For instance, did you give the homeless guy on the train money because you were really led to do so internally or did you want to be noticed by the lady next to you as being a good Samaritan? Doing self-evaluations will help us to keep our egos in check. We will be forced to deal with our true intentions and then begin to make changes as needed. We will learn through checking in on our own selves that we really don't have much time to focus on the wrongs and rights of others. We must keep account of own selves, which is a very time-consuming job.

When doing your self-evaluations, feel free to journal your findings in an effort to track progress or lack thereof. This is also a time when you can connect with your Creator as we discussed earlier. You can begin to evaluate yourself, ask the "whys," and then even request assistance in making changes. Looking in the mirror is not for the faint at heart, but if you are tired of carrying around unwanted SHIT, grab that mirror and do your work.

We can practice self-evaluation below (ONLY if you are completing at a day's end—if not, come back before bed...) What have you done right today? What have you done wrong today? What can you improve to be a better you tomorrow?

_____

_____

_____

_____

_____

_____

_____

_____

_____

_____

_____

_____

_____

_____

_____

_____

18. DON'T BE SO HARD ON YOURSELF

When it is time to deal with ourselves, especially if we have never done it before, it can turn into a bashing session inwardly. We will begin to beat ourselves up because we finally start to see the error of our ways and it doesn't feel good. If we are not careful, we can find ourselves in a cycle of wanting to change but feeling like it's pointless because we are such bad people. This is not true.

We all have messed up in life and guess what—we will continue to mess up in life. There are people who have been given the opportunity of a lifetime, and they blow it because they make a mistake. Oh well, SHIT HAPPENS. We have to learn to bounce back from our mistakes and try our best to learn from them. If we began to focus so much on the "wrongs," we suck the energy from the process of finding out what is right in our lives. Our focus stays planted on the bad, and we so quickly forget about everything else that is working together so beautifully in our lives.

Of course, we should always take the moment to correct ourselves, but as you do so, it is also a must that we affirm ourselves for even having the humility to find self-error. Learn to celebrate you. Stop beating yourself up. Love yourself and embrace every inch of who you are and who you are becoming.

When are the times that you are hardest on yourself? Why?

_____

_____

_____

_____

_____

_____

_____

_____

_____

_____

_____

_____

_____

_____

_____

_____

_____

_____

19. KNOW THAT EVERYONE WON'T LIKE YOU

Growing up, I had this thing where I really wanted people to like me. I wanted it so much that I would find myself doing and saying things just to get their approval. Yes, these were issues that were bred within me because of seeds that were planted in my garden at an early age. However, I didn't put the pieces together at that time. All I knew was that I had a longing to be accepted.

I remember being a part of not just one clique but two cliques. And anyone who knows anything about cliques knows that you are only supposed to have ONE clique that you are loyal too. Nope, not me. During the nineties when I grew up, we had no social media to take our attention. So, we had lots of time and energy to be creative with things, even all the way down to the names of our cliques. With that said, we named our cliques based on each person's name. So, say for instance, we had a "Jane," "Arnold," "Mary," and "Stephanie" in our clique, our collective name would have been "JAMS," as we took the first initial of everyone's name. So, being that I needed to be approved internally, I made sure that my initial was in both of my clique's group names. It brought me so much comfort to know that I was welcomed not only by one group, but two groups. I just knew that I was winning, until one day, I had the blinders lifted from my eyes.

I will never forget that while I thought everyone liked me, I came to realize that there were people that couldn't stand my guts. I remember being so distraught that someone actually didn't like me—OMG! It was then when one of my classmates, whom I didn't really associate with, spoke some words to me that literally changed my life. She walked up to me and it was almost unreal looking back. She said to me, "Everyone is not going to like you," and she seemed to disappear into thin air. Those words changed my perspective of myself and of others (sidebar: she's a therapist now—go figure). From that moment on, I remembered that people have a choice in whether or not they like me, and it is my duty to continue to be who I am regardless.

When dealing with our SHIT, we must not focus on if people like us or not. If they do, great! If they don't, great! Life still must go on. We must understand that if a person is not attracted to our being, there is nothing we could or should do about it. It's their loss— not ours. Though that may sound arrogant, it will help to sooth the bruise on your ego. Trust me.

DEAL WITH YOUR SH!T

How does it feel knowing that there are people that will never be attracted to your energy?

_____

_____

_____

_____

_____

_____

_____

_____

_____

_____

_____

_____

_____

_____

_____

_____

Erika Utley, LPC

20. EMBRACE THAT YOU WILL FOREVER BE EVOLVING

Have you ever met a person that constantly changes their hair, or someone who constantly switches up their career, or a person who changes spouses like they change their underwear? If you have encountered this type of person, you have witnessed evolution in its most simplistic form. For the person I just described, they would typically be thought of as indecisive, flaky, or just plain old childish. However, this person is the person that we should all strive to be.

If you find yourself never changing your way of doing things, this might just be an issue. Without change, there is no true growth. Am I saying to divorce your spouse because you need to evolve? No, I am saying that it may be time to change your interaction with him or her. It may be time to spice up some things if you have been doing the same old routine for the past twenty years. Learning to be okay with evolving takes a lot of courage and fearlessness. When we don't want to deal with our SHIT, it makes it so much more challenging to evolve into a more genuine reflection of yourself.

Our SHIT causes us to live in a state of pain. When we are in pain, evolving into something greater than we are is pretty far-fetched. However, dealing with your SHIT will shorten the process of pain, and before you know it, you will be able to begin to evolve into the person you were truly designed to be. You will be able to live without fear, and living without fear is the breeding ground for personal evolution.

What have you been afraid to change about yourself? What have you been afraid to embrace about yourself?

_____

_____

_____

_____

_____

_____

_____

_____

_____

_____

_____

_____

_____

_____

_____

_____

21. UN-TAME YOUR WILD SIDE (WITHIN REASON)

In the hustle and bustle of life, we must learn to have a good time. We have to learn to let our hair down and partake in some good old-fashioned fun. If your daily routine is "eat, work, sleep, repeat," it may be time to tap into your wild side a little. It is important to do some things that you have always wanted to do, but because your SHIT was in the way, you were too afraid to do.

For instance, maybe you have always wanted to rock climb, but your inner critic told you that you were way too clumsy to do it. Well, now is the time to hush up that inner voice and get out there and have some fun. Or maybe you have always pictured yourself riding a motorcycle, but you never thought that you were coordinated enough to do it. If so, I suggest you take a few courses to learn the ropes, put on your leather chaps, and ride into the sunset. The goal here is not to make careless choices, but to instead take a few risks to embrace the fun side of what life has to offer.

Some of us have gotten so caught up in simply trying to survive that we forget to be adventurous and just enjoy our lives from time to time. Yes, we mustn't forget our main priorities such as going to work or parenting, but we must also not forget that enjoying life is a priority as well. I would be rich if I had a dollar for every time I've heard someone say, "It's like we live to only pay bills." Essentially, this is the lifestyle that many of us have adopted, but that isn't how it has to be. Make time for activities you are interested in and enjoy doing. The same way that we set aside forty-plus hours a week to be clocked in at a job is the same way that we can set aside a few hours to un-tame the adventurous being within us.

We will all one day reach the end of our lives, and it is at that point where we will either feel as though we had a life well-lived or if we never truly lived at all. Make your choice today! There's no use in learning to deal with your SHIT if you won't have at least a little fun while doing it. Live like there was no yesterday and that there probably won't be a tomorrow. Live your life with no regrets!

DEAL WITH YOUR SH!T

What are the things you would want to do if today was your last day living?

_____

_____

_____

_____

_____

_____

_____

_____

_____

_____

_____

_____

_____

_____

_____

_____

22. PACE YOURSELF

Have you ever heard the saying, "Rome wasn't built in a day?" This phrase essentially means that a great work of art takes time to be created. Given that we live in a society where we are able to access almost anything in a short amount of time, we often try to apply this same fast-pace mentality to our own existence. The areas of life that historically took time to complete have now been replaced with more time-efficient processes. For instance, we no longer have to stand over a stove for hours in order to feed our families because we can either pick up our meals from a fast food restaurant or even better, have it delivered right to our doorstep.

This fast and convenient way of doing daily tasks is not at all successful when we talk about doing our own self-work. We are not able to go to a convenience store and purchase a drink that will help to dissolve and resolve our internal issues. We have to put in the work, and it does in fact take time. There is no quick fix in dealing with your SHIT. With that being said, be patient and pace yourself. Take all the time you need to rebuild yourself in order to create your truest work of art within.

If you were to purchase a house and you found out later that the entire building process was done in only 24 hours, I'm sure questions would be raised concerning the quality of the home. Why is this? Well, simply because no one wants a rush job. Apply that same thinking to your own self. Why rush building yourself? Do you really want to walk around knowing that you are a rush job?

Begin to take time to learn each intricate part of you. Learn your likes, dislikes, and those areas of you that you know need to be thrown in the nearest dumpster, never to be seen again. Take time to learn from your mistakes in an effort to not make the same error twice. Spend time with yourself in order to become completely and utterly in tune with who you truly are. Rome wasn't built in a day, so why should you try to build yourself within a day?

DEAL WITH YOUR SH!T

What are some areas of your life in which you need to pace yourself?
What are areas in which you need to learn patience?

_____

_____

_____

_____

_____

_____

_____

_____

_____

_____

_____

_____

_____

_____

_____

_____

Erika Utley, LPC

23. TAKE CARE OF YOUR MACHINE

Mental wellness and physical wellness go hand in hand. Did you know that if you are going through a period of depression that there is a strong possibility that during that time, you may become physically ill as well? Did you also know that going through a time of physical illness can induce mental health challenges? Well, if you didn't know, now you do.

We have to be sure that we are caring for not only our mental health but our physical health as well. When dealing with our SHIT, it's not just a mental detox but a physical detox too. We have to work on taking better care of our machines (aka our bodies) given that they house our minds and spirits. If you are in tune with your body, it will tell you exactly what it needs. Your body will tell you when it needs rest, it will tell you when it needs nourishment, and it will tell you even when it is aroused.

Please note that your physical self and mental self are always in constant communication, so there is not a separation between the two. I would imagine that a conversation between physical and mental would go something like this, "Hey, Physical, looks like today will be a depressed one, so more than likely, you won't be that active" or "Hey, Mental, seems like we had plenty of water, fresh fruits, and veggies today, so you will probably be really happy." Though it may seem funny, this is factual. The body and mind are one in the same. If you take care of one, be sure to take of the other.

89

With that being said, we should look more closely into the foods that we consume into our bodies. There are some foods that naturally boost our mood and some foods that naturally cause us to have a decrease in dopamine (aka our "happy juice"). So if you are already dealing with your SHIT and you decide to partake in a food that is not the most beneficial to you mentally or physically, dealing with your SHIT will be ten times harder on that day. So why not just make healthier food choices? It's easier said than done but begin with baby steps. Also, try to introduce physical activity into your life. This will work wonders for not only your body but for your mental state. Take a jog or do some jumping jacks when you are in the process of dealing with your SHIT. It will definitely make your SHIT removal process a lot smoother. Take care of every part of you in your effort to live your best life.

What are some areas that you could improve upon that relate to your physical well-being?

_____

_____

_____

_____

_____

_____

_____

_____

_____

_____

_____

_____

_____

_____

_____

_____

_____

_____

Erika Utley, LPC

24. LIVE IN LOVE

Some years ago, during a beauty shop girls' talk, the conversation of love came about. Now mind you, I was fairly young at the time and didn't understand half of the topics that the other ladies were discussing, but I do remember one thing. The one thing that I remember that stuck with me was, "In this life, we can either live in love or live in fear." I remember sitting there stuck to the stylist seat and not being able to move because what I had heard was so profound. I thought about the concept for a long time, and eventually, I realized that I had been living in total fear. I was living in fear of other's perceptions of me. I was living in fear of failure. I was living in fear of success. I was living in fear of the past. I was living in fear of the future. I was living in fear of hate. I was living in fear of love. I was just simply living in FEAR.

This is what happens when we don't deal with our SHIT - we live in fear of every aspect of life. We tend to continue to feel victimized instead of feeling victorious. When I decided to deal with my SHIT, I decided to no longer live in fear but to live in LOVE. Living in love means you live a life on a higher frequency and are able to see and experience beyond what the naked eye allows. Living in love will cause you to have an energy that encompasses qualities such as compassion, joy, peace, loyalty, forgiveness, tolerance, respect, generosity, and humility. On the other hand, when we live in fear, our energy is driven by our egos, and we are filled with guilt, regret, jealousy, judgment, greed, arrogance, stubbornness, insecurity, and shame.

When living in love, we understand that every aspect of ourselves is intimately connected to other people and the world around us. With this understanding, we do not see anything separate. We understand that the child we see standing at the bus stop is just as much our child as our own child. We understand that going outside and being able to breathe smoothly wouldn't be possible if the trees were not there. We simply understand the connection and where we fit into this big world.

Living in fear makes us see things separate and we operate based on unrealistic scarcity. We think that we have to compete in order to get what we need because there may just not be enough for everyone. However, remember I said that we were all created with our OWN unique purpose? Because of this, no one will be able to do what you were purposed to do, so there is no competition and there will be enough to go around for everyone. If you have found yourself living in fear up until this point, don't forget that living in LOVE is definitely an option for you. Deal with your SHIT and let that fear become swallowed up by LOVE.

DEAL WITH YOUR SH!T

When are some times that you have lived in fear? What are ways that you can begin to intentionally live in love on a daily basis?

_____

_____

_____

_____

_____

_____

_____

_____

_____

_____

_____

_____

_____

_____

_____

_____

Erika Utley, LPC

25. FLUSH AWAY YOUR EXCUSES

Growing up, there was a quote that was stated at least once per month in my home, and if I could be quite frank, it literally made me cringe every time I heard it. The reason I cringed was that I didn't understand what it meant and why it had to be said so much. That quote was, "It's a great life if you don't weaken."

Now as an adult, I totally grasp the concept and I even find myself silently reciting the quote these days. This phrase basically means that we can have our best life if we choose to stay the course. We must not give in to weaknesses and allow all of our dreams and aspirations to form into SHIT. These weaknesses come in the form of excuses. We must no longer make EXCUSES for ourselves. For so long, we have made excuses to not deal with our SHIT, and it hasn't landed us anywhere but in a tumultuous, emotionally powered, cycle of nothingness.

Making excuses will cause you to lose the very essence of who you were created to be. Excuses allow for justification as to why you are not working on yourself. They also are a direct indication of your lack of accountability for your choices. In the long run, excuses are only hurting the person making them. So as with anything else in life, excuse making is a choice. You can choose to make excuses and prolong your internal healing, or you can put your big girl or big boy drawers on and face the music of your life. The choices are always yours my friend. Remember that excuses are a silent killer, taking every opportunity to draw you further and further away from your destiny. If your goal is to overcome your SHIT, now is the time to FLUSH AWAY ALL OF YOUR EXCUSES.

DEAL WITH YOUR SH!T

What are the excuses that you have made for your life? How do you plan to cut the excuses?

_____

_____

_____

_____

_____

_____

_____

_____

_____

_____

_____

_____

_____

_____

_____

_____

Erika Utley, LPC

26. (BONUS) LET IT GO

This will be the simplest step of them all... Let that SHIT go!

This goes for a person, a job, a situation, etc. If you know that this person, job, or situation is no longer adding life to you, but instead helping to dig your grave daily, it's time to let it go! Or even better, if someone or something wants to exit from your life, let it go. We will no longer beg for someone or something to stay that does not want to be there. If you do this, you are not only saying that you are desperate, but more importantly, you scream that you are full of SHIT.

Dealing with your SHIT will allow you to open the door as far as you can and let whatever it is that wants to walk, walk straight up out your life, and you will be totally okay with it! Work on you and understand that if it can leave, it was never a part of your permanent tree of life. LET IT GO my friends!

What are some situations or who are some people that you need to let go of right now? Why?

_____

_____

_____

_____

_____

_____

_____

_____

_____

_____

_____

_____

_____

_____

_____

_____

CONCLUSION

So, you have made it through the 25 (plus added bonus) ways to overcome your shame, hurt, insecurities, and trials. I must admit, I am proud of you for taking the first step in DEALING with your SHIT. Please note that this is only the beginning of a lifelong process of healing and internal evolution. Commit to yourself to never stop working on YOU. Find peace in knowing that all of the answers you need are somewhere deep within - you never have to search too far. I encourage you to feel, be, and do all that you were created to feel, be, and do. Don't leave any page unturned in your life. Grab on to the pieces of you and continue to work diligently to put the beautiful puzzle of your life together. Just remember to always deal with your SHIT before it begins to deal with you.

DEAL
with YOUR
SH!T

Journal YOUR Journey in the pages ahead...

JOURNAL YOUR JOURNEY

In the pages ahead, you will find the following journaling activities to complete over the course of a year:

-52 week Self Affirmation Log:

For each week (52 weeks), write <u>1</u> self affirmation and recite it daily for that entire week.

-12 month SHIT Dealing Tracker:

For each month (12 months), journal about how you plan to deal with your SHIT during that time-frame. Once you have completed the task, jot down the date it was completely dealt with.

Don't cheat yourself---DO YOUR WORK!!!

Enjoy...

Affirmation Log (Week 1-18)

1. _____
2. _____
3. _____
4. _____
5. _____
6. _____
7. _____
8. _____
9. _____
10. _____
11. _____
12. _____
13. _____
14. _____
15. _____
16. _____
17. _____
18. _____

Affirmation Log (Week 19-36)

19. _____

20. _____

21. _____

22. _____

23. _____

24. _____

25. _____

26. _____

27. _____

28. _____

29. _____

30. _____

31. _____

32. _____

33. _____

34. _____

35. _____

36. _____

Affirmation Log (Week 37-52)

37. _____

38. _____

39. _____

40. _____

41. _____

42. _____

43. _____

44. _____

45. _____

46. _____

47. _____

48. _____

49. _____

50. _____

51. _____

52. _____

SHIT Dealing Tracker

Month 1

This month, I will DEAL with My SHIT by...

_____

_____

_____

_____

_____

_____

_____

_____

_____

_____

_____

_____

_____

_____

SHIT GOT DEALT with on: _____

Date

SHIT Dealing Tracker

Month 2

This month, I will DEAL with My SHIT by...

_____

_____

_____

_____

_____

_____

_____

_____

_____

_____

_____

_____

_____

SHIT GOT DEALT with on: _____

Date

SHIT Dealing Tracker

Month 3

This month, I will DEAL with My SHIT by...

_____

_____

_____

_____

_____

_____

_____

_____

_____

_____

_____

_____

_____

_____

SHIT GOT DEALT with on: _____

Date

SHIT Dealing Tracker

Month 4

This month, I will DEAL with My SHIT by...

_____

_____

_____

_____

_____

_____

_____

_____

_____

_____

_____

_____

SHIT GOT DEALT with on: _____

Date

SHIT Dealing Tracker

Month 5

This month, I will DEAL with My SHIT by...

_____

_____

_____

_____

_____

_____

_____

_____

_____

_____

_____

_____

_____

SHIT GOT DEALT with on: _____

Date

SHIT Dealing Tracker

Month 6

This month, I will DEAL with My SHIT by...

_____

_____

_____

_____

_____

_____

_____

_____

_____

_____

_____

_____

_____

_____

_____

SHIT GOT DEALT with on: _____

Date

SHIT Dealing Tracker

Month 7

This month, I will DEAL with My SHIT by...

_____

_____

_____

_____

_____

_____

_____

_____

_____

_____

_____

_____

_____

SHIT GOT DEALT with on: _____

Date

SHIT Dealing Tracker

Month 8

This month, I will DEAL with My SHIT by...

_____

_____

_____

_____

_____

_____

_____

_____

_____

_____

_____

_____

_____

_____

_____

SHIT GOT DEALT with on: _____

Date

SHIT Dealing Tracker

Month 9

This month, I will DEAL with My SHIT by...

_____

_____

_____

_____

_____

_____

_____

_____

_____

_____

_____

_____

_____

SHIT GOT DEALT with on: _____

Date

SHIT Dealing Tracker

Month 10

This month, I will DEAL with My SHIT by...

_____

_____

_____

_____

_____

_____

_____

_____

_____

_____

_____

_____

_____

_____

SHIT GOT DEALT with on: _____

Date

SHIT Dealing Tracker

Month 11

This month, I will DEAL with My SHIT by...

_____

_____

_____

_____

_____

_____

_____

_____

_____

_____

_____

_____

SHIT GOT DEALT with on: _____

Date

SHIT Dealing Tracker

Month 12

This month, I will DEAL with My SHIT by...

_____

_____

_____

_____

_____

_____

_____

_____

_____

_____

_____

_____

_____

_____

SHIT GOT DEALT with on: _____

Date

CONGRATULATIONS

Congrats on finally DEALING with Your SHIT!!!

Thank you for trusting me to guide you on this journey! My hope is that you will kick the SHIT to the curb and truly begin to SMILE from within...

Until next time,

Erika ("The Smileologist")

88613230R00074

Made in the USA
Columbia, SC
01 February 2018